THE STRONG DELUSION

GODS JUDGMENT ON THE MINDS THAT REJECT THE TRUTH

BY MONTE L. MONK

Copyright © 2025 by Monte Monk
All rights reserved.

No part of this publication may be reproduced, distributed, or transmitted in any form or by any means, including photocopying, recording, or other electronic or mechanical methods, without the prior written permission of the publisher, except in the case of brief quotations embodied in critical reviews and certain other noncommercial uses permitted by copyright law.

For permission requests, write to the publisher at:
Judah Media Publishing
2509 Hyacinth Dr, Mesquite, TX 75181
info@judhamediallc.com

This is a work of nonfiction. Unless otherwise noted, all scripture quotations are taken from the [Version of Bible, e.g., King James Version], in the public domain. Any reference to real people, events, or places is used factually and with respect.

Cover design by Judah Media
ISBN: ISBN: 978-1-7372539-2-1

Printed in the United States of America

First Edition

I give my deepest appreciation to my lovely wife Teresa who has stood and yet stands with me through prayer, love and providing constant encouragement through tough times.

Table of Contents

Introduction

1. The Psychological View of Delusion------7
2. The Theological View of Delusion---------17
3. The Sociological View of Delusion--------25
4. The Satanic Origin of Delusion-------------35
5. The Demonic Role in Delusion-------------51
6. The Demonization of Social Media--------57
7. Delusion and The Demonization-----------65 of the Mind
8. The Falling Away and----------------------78 the Mystery of Iniquity
9. The Word Made Flesh----------------------88
10. Escaping The Judgment Of Delusion------98
11. The Importance of Fellowship--------------107 In Escaping The Judgment Of Delusion
12. The Strong Delusion Workbook------------113

Bibliography

INTRODUCTION

Driven by political ambition and a strong desire to affirm his authority over Israel, King Ahab decided to go to war against the Arameans and claim the city of Ramoth-Gilead as a prize. His motivations for this action were entangled in pride and his hunger for glory. In his conquest, he called upon King Jehoshaphat to assist. And to assure King Jehoshaphat of victory, he called upon his order of advisors and prophets, who stated that God was with him and that his ambitious campaign would be victorious.

> *Then the king of Israel gathered the prophets together, about four hundred men, and said unto them, Shall I go against Ramoth-Gilead to battle, or shall I forbear? And they said, go up; for the Lord shall deliver it into the hand of the king. 1 Kings 22:6*

But King Jehoshaphat was unconvinced and asked if there was a prophet of the Lord. King Ahab explicitly stated that there was, but he hated him because he only prophesied evil to him. He did not speak the words that King Ahab wanted to hear. At Jehoshaphat's request to hear from a prophet of the Lord, Micaiah, was summoned.

When Micaiah arrived and was inquired by King Ahab to tell him if he would be victorious if he went up to Ramoth Gilead, Micaiah first mocked the prophets by agreeing with them. But King Ahab, knowing his true character and stance, inquired of him again and told him to speak only what the Lord said to him. Micaiah's response:

> *And he said, I saw all Israel scattered upon the hills, as sheep that have not a shepherd: and the Lord said,* **These** *have no master: let them return every man to his house in peace. 1 Kings 22:17.*

These words displeased the king, and he responded to King Jehoshaphat, saying:

> Did I not tell thee that he would prophesy no good concerning me, but evil? – 1 Kings 22:18

King Ahab stubbornly sought out voices that affirmed his desires rather than those that warned with truth. Though given every opportunity to hear the voice of God through the prophet Micaiah, Ahab willfully chose to believe a lie. He wanted war.

Because he decided to abort the truth, God gave him over to the lies spoken to him by the false prophets. The source of the prophecies spoken came through a lying spirit that God allowed to fill the mouths of the false prophets. As a result, Ahab went up to battle and he died.

King Ahab became delusional out of pride, ambition, and selfishness. He wanted to win and take the city so badly that when the words of the prophet Micaiah provided him with clear evidence that he would lose the battle, he "denied" the truth and held onto a false belief that later cost him his life.

Where did God's Judgement come in? God allowed a lying spirit to fill the mouths of false prophets, sealing King Ahab in that false belief without the option of redemption. This was the result of his constant rejection of the truth.

> And the Lord said, Who shall persuade Ahab, that he may go up and fall at Ramoth-gilead? And one said on this manner, and another said on that manner. And there came forth a spirit, and stood before the Lord, and said, I will persuade him. And the Lord said unto him, Wherewith? And he said, I will go forth, and I will be a lying spirit in the mouth of all his prophets. And he said, Thou shalt persuade him, and prevail also: go forth, and do so. Now therefore, behold, the Lord hath put a lying spirit in the mouth of all these thy prophets, and

> the Lord hath spoken evil concerning thee. 1 Kings 22:20-23

The same spirit of Ahab rules today—a spirit that demands prophets speak "smooth things" (Isaiah 30:10), preferring the comfort of delusion over the cost of repentance. The danger is not only for the openly rebellious but also for believers who selectively receive the parts of God's Word they find palatable, rejecting the fullness of His counsel.

The bible warns us of a future where false prophets will arise and come "in his name," aligning themselves with God and Jesus Christ, claiming to be filled with the Spirit of God, and will deceive many (St. Matthew 24:5). Their ability to deceive many will not only be due to "gullibility". Their power will be magnified due to a mass rejection of the truth of God's word. God has already stated that because many will reject the truth, he will do the same thing he did to King Ahab to those who refuse to believe. And that is to give them over to believe a lying spirit, sealing them in a false belief that will result in no opportunity for redemption.

> Even him, whose coming is after the working of Satan with all power and signs and lying wonders, And with all deceivableness of unrighteousness in them that perish; because they received not the love of the truth, that they

> might be saved. And for this cause God shall
> send them strong delusion, that they should
> believe a lie: That they all might be damned
> who believed not the truth, but had pleasure in
> unrighteousness. 2 Thessalonians 2:9-12

Even now, we are seeing people reject the truth of God's word and validate men and women who claim to be prophets of God by faithful attendance at their services, subscribing to and following them on various social media platforms. If one were to call out these teachers and so-called prophets on deception, they would be quickly bombarded with rude statements and scriptures that defend the false teacher.

This phenomenon is not limited to the church world; it's also seen in the political ranks. Many are so blindly dedicated to their political parties that they are willing to sacrifice biblical values for voting in their party's delegate.

I believe that this judgment is happening now. We are living and seeing this judgment play out right before our eyes. The hand of God's wrath has already begun moving throughout the land, and the next events, I believe, we are about to see are the rapture of the church and the rise of the Antichrist to power. In this book, " The Strong Delusion", I will teach you how delusion works, how to recognize it in the world, the church, and maybe in a friend, so that you can call it out, and become a stronger witness for Christ, bring about deliverance, and maybe for yourself, "AVOID THE JUDGEMENT OF GOD".

Chapter One

The Psychological View of Delusion

> "And for this cause God shall send them strong delusion, that they should believe a lie." — 2 Thessalonians 2:11 (KJV)

Throughout the ages, humanity has grappled with the concepts of truth and reality. Yet the Scriptures reveal that deception is not merely a matter of confusion or ignorance; it is a moral and spiritual rebellion against God's revealed truth. The psychological and theological dimensions of delusion form the very foundation of the crisis we face right now in the world, the church, and even our personal lives. This chapter examines how delusion operates in the mind, which is the heart of man, and why understanding its nature is crucial to recognizing the hour of judgment in which we live.

Modern psychology, as documented in the *Diagnostic and Statistical Manual of Mental Disorders (DSM-5)*, defines delusion as a firmly held false belief despite clear contradictory evidence. Delusions often involve the misinterpretation of reality itself — a persistent distortion that remains impervious to correction, reason, or evidence.

In clinical settings, delusions are associated with severe psychiatric conditions, including

- schizophrenia,
- delusional disorder,
- bipolar disorder.

Examples may range from:

- paranoid delusions (believing one is being persecuted without cause) to
- grandiose delusions (believing one possesses supernatural abilities or divine status). More on this later...

In psychological terms, delusion is seen as a cognitive fracture—a failure of the mind to interpret reality correctly. It results from dysfunctional processes that evaluate truth, evidence, and logical coherence. An example would be a person who continues to believe in a conspiracy despite the overwhelming evidence presented to him that contradicts it and proves that the conspiracy is a lie.

Cognitive Dissonance

Why does this happen?

"Cognitive dissonance." The fundamental psychological phenomenon where an individual experiences profound mental discomfort, emotional stress, and internal tension when confronted with two contradictory beliefs, or when new information directly challenges their existing worldview. The human psyche intrinsically craves consistency and internal harmony, and this drive for psychological stability prompts a powerful, often unconscious, need to resolve such conflicts.

To alleviate this uncomfortable state, the mind frequently employs various defense mechanisms. Rather than confronting a difficult truth that might necessitate repentance, personal change, or an admission of error, the individual may instinctively cling to existing falsehoods. This often involves rationalizing the conflicting information, twisting it to fit pre-existing notions, or even outright rejecting it. This cognitive maneuver serves to protect the ego and self-identity, preventing the individual from feeling like a failure or being accountable.

The insidious nature of this process lies in its ability to reinforce delusion, turning an inconvenient truth into a perceived threat that must be avoided at all costs, thereby solidifying the false belief as a psychological shield against the discomfort of being wrong or morally responsible.

Ego-Protection

The human mind is equipped with a defense mechanism designed to preserve an individual's self-image, perceived integrity, and internal sense of consistency. This psychological phenomenon, known as ego suppression or ego defense, acts as an automatic guardian, swiftly denying, rationalizing, or minimizing information that challenges these core aspects.

When truth penetrates too deeply, threatening the carefully constructed sense of self, the ego "instinctively" recoils, perceiving the truth not as a liberating force but as a direct assault that must be deflected to ward off mental discomfort and maintain cognitive harmony. This reflexive act can even extend to projecting blame onto the source of the challenging information.

However, a purely psychological framework, with its naturalistic focus on the brain and environment, often falls short in fully explaining the depths of human deception. Scripture offers a more comprehensive understanding, positing that at the root of this mental resistance lies spiritual corruption.

> The heart (the mind) is <u>deceitful</u> above all things, and <u>desperately wicked:</u> who can know it? Jeremiah 17:9

This suggests that the mind's tendency to suppress truth is not merely a cognitive malfunction but a manifestation of a deeper moral and spiritual inclination.

This perspective aligns with Paul's assertion in Romans 1:18, where he states that people "hold the truth in unrighteousness. The reek word katech , meaning to hold down" or "suppress," conveys a deliberate and conscious rejection of what is known to be true. It implies that individuals do not suppress truth because they are ignorant of it, but rather because they fundamentally *refuse to be governed by it*. This points to a resistance that transcends simple intellectual dissonance, evolving into an active spiritual rebellion against divine authority.

Therefore, delusion does not arise in a vacuum or solely from a benign mental malfunction. Instead, it originates from this profound internal conflict: the human mind's encounter with a truth that directly threatens its established, often comfortable, constructed reality. Rather than embracing a challenging truth that might demand repentance, significant change, or humble submission, the individual consciously or unconsciously rationalizes the lie. This deliberate embrace of deception transforms the lie into a psychological shield, protecting against the discomfort of accountability, the fear of being wrong, and the perceived threat of humbling oneself before a higher truth.

If left unchecked, this act of suppression can escalate beyond mere psychological defense, evolving into a state of profound spiritual blindness and, ultimately, a form of divine judgment where individuals are given over to the very deceptions they cling to.

Delusion does not emerge in a vacuum. It begins with internal conflict—the human mind's encounter with a truth that threatens its constructed sense of reality. When truth confronts the lie a person has built their life around, the mind reacts defensively. This reaction is more than confusion or ignorance; it is a process of suppression, rooted in cognitive dissonance and ego protection, and—if left unchecked—it becomes an act of divine judgment.

Suppression Becomes Judgment.

The initial psychological discomfort ignited by confronting truth prompts the human mind to reinterpret reality in a manner that alleviates emotional strain. Over time, this deliberate reinterpretation solidifies into a deeply entrenched delusional framework—a comprehensive cognitive system wherein falsehoods are not merely embraced as true but become absolutely essential for psychological survival. In a clinical sense, this process precisely defines a delusional disorder: the unwavering adherence to a fixed, false belief, even in the face of overwhelming and undeniable contradictory evidence. This is a powerful illustration of the mind's capacity to build its own prison, where the perceived safety of a lie outweighs the challenging freedom of truth.

However, the Word of God reveals that this descent into delusion is far more than a mere psychological aberration; it carries profound spiritual and judicial implications. The Apostle Paul, in his letter to the Romans, unveils a solemn truth:

> And even as they did not like to retain God in their knowledge, God gave them over to a reprobate mind, to do those things which are not convenient - Romans 1:28

This passage teaches us *that persistent, willful suppression of divine truth* eventually leads to a divine consequence. It is a terrifying reality that those who continuously reject God's revelation can be, by His righteous judgment, relinquished to their own corrupted understanding.

The Greek word for "reprobate" *adokimos*, carries significant weight. It literally means "unapproved, unexamined, unfit, or worthless," often used in the context of metals that, when tested, are found to be impure and rejected. Spiritually, it signifies a mind that has become so corrupted by its own refusal of truth that it is no longer capable of discerning between right and wrong, between reality and deception. It is a mind that, through its own choices, has rendered itself useless for comprehending divine things, akin to a spoiled fruit or a coin that fails to pass inspection.

This "giving over" is not an arbitrary act of vengeance from heaven, but a solemn and terrifying withdrawal of divine truth and restraint. When individuals consistently turn away from the word of God, God, in His sovereignty, permits them to walk in the darkness they have chosen. The very mind that once experienced the jarring friction of cognitive dissonance, struggling between truth and falsehood, eventually reaches a point where it feels no such discomfort. The conscience, once sensitive, becomes "seared with a hot iron" (1 Timothy 4:2, KJV), losing its ability to register moral alarm.

> Speaking lies in hypocrisy; having their conscience seared with a hot iron; - 1 Timothy 4:2

In this tragic state, the delusion, once a mere coping mechanism, morphs into an unshakeable identity. The lies that were initially embraced for comfort become the very fabric of one's perceived reality, leaving no room for repentance or genuine transformation.

CHAPTER TWO

THE THEOLOGICAL VIEW OF DELUSION

> While it is said, Today if ye will hear his voice,
> harden not your hearts, as in the provocation.
> Hebrews 3:15

Theologically, delusion occurs when someone rejects divine truth and stubbornly clings to a lie. This act goes beyond what is defined as human error and is an act of "spiritual rebellion." Instead of yielding and accepting the truth of God's word, the hearer clings to their own rules, values, and morals, compromising the truth of God's word or responding in all-out rebellion.

In either case, the hearer serves their personal desires, which is the core of idolatry. They engage in false worship of the self, comfort, and sin. The interpretation of truth stems from individual thought, defining right from wrong without God. Self is placed on a pedestal, and personal ease and gratification are used to suppress any form of discomfort, which ultimately leads to the justification of sin, iniquity, and immorality.

The mind of the self then begins to shape the individual's worldview and reality, leading them down a path opposite of God's holy way into a distorted reality constructed on the foundation of unbelief and fleshly impulses. The individual becomes a god to himself, serving his creature over the one true "creator.".

> "Who changed the truth of God into a lie, and worshipped and served the creature more than the Creator, who is blessed for ever. Amen."
> Romans 1:25

This is an insidious deconstruction of the soul and mind of an individual who refuses to accept the truth, especially when defending against the truth with a false belief. It's not a matter of differing opinions warring against one another. It's deeper than that. It's actually a fundamental shift in authority. In this case, spiritual authority. Personal validation becomes the measure of truth not the word of God.

> All scripture is given by inspiration of God, and is profitable for doctrine, for reproof, for correction, for instruction in righteousness: 2 Timothy 3:16

Pride & Obstinate: The symptoms of Delusion

Prideful and obstinate are two character traits that can be rooted deep in an individual's heart and soul, proving that delusion is not a mere external assault on the mind. When these two traits begin to harden, coupled with a rejection of the truth of the word of God, a delusion of the spirit is not too far behind. Unrepentant pride and obstinacy eventually lead to being enslaved by it.

The Nature of Pride

The core of "pride" is self-exaltation over anything and anyone, including God, truth, and correction. When pride is at work, it mocks, ridicules, and even reinterprets the truth, often leading to a "misinterpretation and hard downfall.

When pride speaks, it convinces the individual that they:

- Know better.
- Don't need to change.
- Can create their "own truth."

It blinds minds and corrupts the soul to the point where, if it's not checked through repentance, it leads to the impossibility of receiving correction. Pride makes the individual see no need to be sorry for their actions. The individual is always right, manifesting snobbiness and arrogance, exaggerating one's own abilities and importance while ignoring and belittling the opinions of others.

The snobbiness and arrogance are traits of a haughty spirit. When people are prideful, they refuse to admit mistakes and respond almost always condescendingly, simply because they have an excessively high opinion of themselves and a sense of entitlement. They overestimate their abilities and importance in the face of others they deem less significant. These individuals suffer from what's called "delusions of grandeur." In the case of religion or Christianity, they feel that their relationship with God, connection with the church, or hierarchical leadership puts them in a position of power and authority.

Their grandiose delusions usually result in impaired judgments, risky behaviors, broken relationships, and social interactions that make it difficult to operate in everyday life.

> Pride goeth before destruction, and an haughty spirit before a fall." Proverbs 16:18

Obstinate

Another symptom of delusion is being "obstinate". An obstinate individual is stubbornly persistent in clinging to a viewpoint, purpose, or action and will resist anyone or anything who attempts to deter them from that purpose, viewpoint, or action. No matter what contrary evidence you provide to prove that they are wrong, they will become more and more inflexible and resist.

Their attitudes are unyielding, and they stand firm against reason, truth, and persuasion. A perfect example of this is the pharaoh of Egypt in Exodus Chapter 8. When God sent a message to let His people go, along with plagues to prove that he was the God of the Israelites, Pharaoh hardened his heart and refused

---

And the Lord spake unto Moses, Go unto Pharaoh, and say unto him, Thus saith the Lord, Let my people go, that they may serve me. And if thou refuse to let them go, behold, I will smite all thy borders with frogs: And the river shall bring forth frogs abundantly, which shall go up and come into thine house, and into thy bedchamber, and upon thy bed, and into the house of thy servants, and upon thy people, and into thine ovens, and into thy kneadingtroughs: And the frogs shall come up both on thee, and upon thy people, and upon all thy servants. And the Lord spake unto Moses, Say unto Aaron, Stretch forth thine hand with thy rod over the streams, over the rivers, and over the ponds, and cause frogs to come up upon the land of Egypt. And Aaron stretched out his hand over the waters of Egypt; and the frogs came up, and covered the land of Egypt. And the magicians did so with their enchantments, and brought up frogs upon the land of Egypt. Then Pharaoh called for Moses and Aaron, and said, Intreat the Lord, that he may take away the frogs from me, and from my people; and I will let the people go, that they may do sacrifice unto the Lord. And Moses said unto Pharaoh, Glory over me: when shall I intreat for thee, and for thy servants, and for thy people, to destroy the frogs from thee and thy houses, that they may remain in the river only? And he said, To morrow. And he said, Be it according to thy

> word: that thou mayest know that there is none like unto the Lord our God. And the frogs shall depart from thee, and from thy houses, and from thy servants, and from thy people; they shall remain in the river only. And Moses and Aaron went out from Pharaoh, and Moses cried unto the Lord because of the frogs which he had brought against Pharaoh. And the Lord did according to the word of Moses; and the frogs died out of the houses, out of the villages, and out of the fields. And they gathered them together upon heaps: and the land stank. But when Pharaoh saw that there was respite, he hardened his heart, and hearkened not unto them; as the Lord had said. Exodus 8:1-15

When the heart is stubborn against God and His truth, it will not remain empty. Like the pharaoh of Egypt, the heart will be filled with deception, creating a false reality against the reality of the one true God. The individual deceives themselves with their "own" righteousness and authority. How many people today, whom you may know, have seen and experienced the power of God, witnessed his miracles, and no doubt have tasted and understood His truth. But after falling away from grace, no matter how hard you witness to them or correct them, they refuse to hear and receive, and will responds with a condescending rebuttal?

When the word of truth is preached, witnessed, or taught to any individual, and they continue to persist on a course of action in thought or deed that is opposite of the word of God, they are not only headed for a fall, but they will not be able to rise again.

> He, that being often reproved hardeneth his neck, shall suddenly be destroyed, and that without remedy. Proverbs 29:1

Chapter Three

The Sociological View of Delusion

In sociology, false beliefs and ideas are widely accepted and reinforced, especially within social groups and cultures that contradict factual evidence and logical reasoning. When false beliefs and ideas are fortified on a massive scale, a collective delusion is formed, leading to widespread dysfunctional and harmful behavior.

When dysfunctional and harmful behavior based on delusion is widespread and embedded into reality through human interaction, it can become a social norm. Even though the ideas and beliefs are false, they will yield real consequences due to ignoring warning signals and contradictory evidence.

As a result, groups that hold onto these false beliefs and ideas can be led into taking dangerous actions and making poor decisions when faced with events that pose a real threat, and vice versa. They can become overly concerned and exaggerate events, spreading panic and fear, or be so unconcerned that when necessary, action is required, it's ignored, and the result is catastrophic and possibly deadly.

We have seen this throughout history in cult ideologies, those who follow conspiracy theories, and racial superiority doctrines. But what's most deceptive about this form of delusion and any other, for that matter, is that these false ideas and beliefs within the groups that hold them provide a "false sense of comfort" in uncertain times. A comfort that is so peaceful or motivating that they are willing to die for it.

The Salem Witch Trials and Delusion

Consider the Salem witch trials. The Puritan community in Salem, Massachusetts, fell under heavy stress due to recent outbreaks of smallpox, raids from the native Americans, economic instability, and internal conflicts that rose throughout their villages. Described as strange behavior and mainly among young girls, symptoms of hysteria, such as convulsions, screaming, and hallucinations, combined with psychological, social, and cultural factors, contributed to the development of a collective delusion.

The Puritan community interpreted these anxieties and unusual behaviors as witchcraft or demonic activity. They ignored the idea that the young girls of that time and community were marginalized and had little power in their political and religious arena. Additionally, there was factionalism, fights over property rights, and local feuds that often involved families, stemming from loyalties to certain leaders. These things created anxieties within the community among children and adolescents, who were heavily susceptible to subconscious mimicking.

Another contributing factor was that in the Puritan society, emotional expression was heavily suppressed, especially in girls and women. This created a severe inner conflict of emotions that soon manifested bodily and was interpreted as spiritual. They were suffering psychogenic illnesses. If a woman cried out, had a seizure, muttered, and even during childbearing experienced mood swings and had a cycle of menstruation, she was viewed as unclean, unnatural, and linked to spiritual dangers, defined as possession or under a spell of witchcraft.

Seeing that the puritans believed that they were living in the last days, Satan and his demons operating in the world, and the lingering old European beliefs about magic and curses being prevalent in their New England society, they considered the scripture taught in Exodus 22:18 that said, " Thou shalt not suffer a witch to live," and felt an urgency to root out all evil.

The religious authority, which was made up of men, accused individuals of witchcraft. A small portion of the accused were men. In contrast, the larger portion of the accused were unmarried women, widowed, lived independent lives, or "owned property" and defied the puritan cultural and gender roles. Easy targets among the accused were outspoken, mentally ill, and even the poor. Midwives, herbalists, and those who had medical knowledge were also accused of practicing witchcraft.

The collective delusion that preyed upon the citizens of Salem was so widespread that many were blinded to the underlying fact that jealousy, land disputes, and family feuds drove the majority of the accusations. Pushed through fear, the trials were about power and control and were used to eliminate rivals. If men defended women during the time of the trials, they too were accused of witchcraft. From 1692 to 1693, 200 people were accused of witchcraft. Twenty died, nineteen people were hanged, and one was tortured to death. One hundred forty-one were women and fifty-two were men. This delusion reflected heavy gender bias through the religious fears of that time.

Modern Day Cults and Delusion

The times we live in now are not much different from those of Salem.

Category	Salem, 1692	Modern Times (Cults, Politics, Tribulation)
Crisis & Social Unrest	Smallpox outbreaks, Native American raids, and internal village conflict	Pandemics, terrorism, mass shootings, economic instability, and global unrest
Psychological Stress	Widespread anxiety, fear of damnation,	Trauma from media overload, isolation, identity confusion, and mental health crisis

	repression of emotion	
Religious Extremism	Literal use of Exodus 22:18 to justify executions	Cults and governments weaponize scripture or ideology to control behavior and punish dissent
Marginalized Victims	Widows, midwives, poor women, and the mentally ill were accused of witchcraft	Whistleblowers, Christians, and politically "incorrect" voices are silenced or labeled dangerous
Charismatic Authority	Male religious leaders controlled accusations and trials	Cult leaders, political influencers, and global elites sway masses with persuasive rhetoric
Gender Bias	The majority of the accused were women who defied traditional gender roles.	Women still face bias; those rejecting progressive norms are ostracized or labeled as regressive.
Scapegoating & Groupthink	Land disputes and rivalries drove accusations.	Ideological cancel culture, partisan demonization, racial and religious scapegoating
False Accusations	Hysteria led to over 200 accused, 20 executed.	Social media mobs, false narratives, and disinformation campaigns destroy reputations and careers.
Spiritual Delusion	The belief that demonic forces were infiltrating society	Rise of New Age mysticism, false prophets, Antichrist system during

		the Tribulation (2 Thess. 2:11)
Suppression of Truth	Dissenters risked accusation and death.	Biblical truth is ridiculed; standing for Christ will bring persecution (Matthew 24:9)

Among the Puritans, the supposed righteous community, seeds of jealousy, authoritarianism, malice, and religious hypocrisy rose and caused unnecessary death in the name of God. The word of God warns us of a timeframe marked as dangerous, complex, and filled with uncertainty.

> This know also, that in the last days perilous times shall come. For men shall be lovers of their own selves, covetous, boasters, proud, blasphemers, disobedient to parents, unthankful, unholy, Without natural affection, trucebreakers, false accusers, incontinent, fierce, despisers of those that are good, Traitors, heady, highminded, lovers of pleasures more than lovers of God; Having a form of godliness, but denying the power thereof: from such turn away. 2 Timothy 3:1-5

Like Salem, perilous times will be marked by widespread moral and spiritual failure due to self-centeredness, rejection of the truth, and resistance to genuine Godliness. Those who are lovers of themselves more than lovers of God will be filled with self-love that promotes self-idolatry, sensuality, emotionalism, and a false spirituality. They will be resistant to Godly authority, becoming extremely evil, deceiving themselves and others.

Their rejection of the truth of God's word will lead them to become prideful and develop or adopt an alternative spirituality, embracing contradictory truths. These truths will be so convincing that they will seduce many from the true faith in Jesus Christ.

> Now the Spirit speaketh expressly, that in the latter times some shall depart from the faith, giving heed to seducing spirits, and doctrines of devils; 1 Timothy 4:1

Modern Day Occultic Belief

When other false truths are accepted over the word of God, occultism is adopted as a replacement. Some of these practices include, but are not limited to:

- Astrology
- Tarot
- Crystals
- Divination

- Spiritism
- Energy Manipulation
- Ritual Magic

These occult practices are seductive in the sense that they offer "hidden knowledge (gnosis)" and, in some cases, provide mystical experiences and self-deification. You are your own god! You control your destiny and bear the power to manifest "your own reality". Again, serving the creature, more than the creator. When the truth of the bible is traded for "personal empowerment", the result is divorce from God into a state of spiritual delusion.

Chapter Four

The Satanic Origin Of Delusion

An individual just doesn't spontaneously become delusional. It's an insidious and subtle scheme in a game of spiritual chess, a deceptive strategy that's played on the battlefield of the mind of those targeted by Satan and his demons for eternal destruction. They sow seeds of doubt, twist the perceptions of God's truth into complex "forms of unbelief" that result in spiritual ruin and everlasting condemnation. Satan is the originator and master influencer of the delusional mind.

> ye are of your father the devil, and the lusts of your father ye will do. He was a murderer from the beginning, and abode not in the truth, because there is no truth in him. When he speaketh a lie, he speaketh of his own: for he is a liar, and the father of it. St. John 8:44

A symptom of a delusional and ungodly condition is to speak and believe lies. To speak a lie according to scripture indicates that one is participating in the "lineage of deception". In the realm of spirituality, if one speaks it, more than likely they believe it, and if they do not, as is the position of some, that yet qualifies them as a deceiver.

The Origin of Deception - Lucifer

Delusion began with Lucifer's fall, a symptom and direct consequence of his pride, which also entailed his beauty and wisdom, thus corrupting his mission and purpose. Lucifer, being lifted in pride, assumed he was just as good and powerful as Almighty God, his Creator. But viewed God as a distortion of what is right and acceptable.

> How art thou fallen from heaven, O Lucifer, son of the morning! how art thou cut down to the ground, which didst weaken the nations! <u>For thou hast said in thine heart, I will ascend into heaven, I will exalt my throne above the stars of God: I will sit also upon the mount of the congregation, in the sides of the north: I will ascend above the heights of the clouds; I will be like the most High</u>. Yet thou shalt be brought down to hell, to the sides of the pit.
> Isaiah 14:12-15

Before it became man's dwelling place, the earth was occupied by angels, who were created to worship God. Lucifer, compared to King Tyrus, was one among many chosen and anointed from the midst of the cherubim angels to represent God on Earth. God created in him the ability to not only make music but to become worship, "personified in a vessel". He was the summation of God's power given to him. He was described as perfect in beauty, reaching its maximum. When it came to power and influence, he had reached his highest heights, unparalleled by any.

> Son of man, take up a lamentation upon the king of Tyrus, and say unto him, Thus saith the Lord GOD; Thou sealest up the sum, full of wisdom, and perfect in beauty. Thou hast been in Eden the garden of God; every precious stone was thy covering, the sardius, topaz, and the diamond, the beryl, the onyx, and the jasper, the sapphire, the emerald, and the carbuncle, and gold: the workmanship of thy tabrets and of thy pipes was prepared in thee in the day that thou wast created. Ezekiel 28:12-13

In this magnificent creation of God, there was "wisdom." Wisdom is more than knowledge, which is awareness of facts, familiarity with situations, and practice of skills. Wisdom, as it relates to God, is the ability to make sound judgments and decisions according to God's divine knowledge.

Lucifer understood the nature and desires of his angelic audience. Because of God's anointing, he was aware of their experiences and patterns of behavior. As the receiver and deliverer of God's word and charged as the angel who covered the very throne of God, he was well attuned to God's will and delivered whatever message was given to him by God to the holy angels. He was perfect until "iniquity" was found in him.

> Thou art the anointed cherub that covereth; and I have set thee so: thou wast upon the holy mountain of God; thou hast walked up and down in the midst of the stones of fire. Thou wast perfect in thy ways from the day that thou wast created, till iniquity was found in thee.
> Ezekiel 28:14-15

When Lucifer challenged God, he had convinced himself that his will would supersede or put him on an equal playing field with God. Jesus testified to the outcome of the battle and Lucifer's defeat

> And he said unto them, I beheld Satan as lightning fall from heaven – St. Luke 10:18

It was at this point that he became "Satan", the adversary or accuser. Satan is not his name, but is a description of who he is, his character, purpose, and mission, which is to oppose everything that is "God". His very nature is to deceive, by stealing, killing, and destroying the testimony of all in the kingdom of God and His entire creation, including those who have denied Christ. The end goal of this work is "ETERNAL SEPARATION FROM GOD"! Let's break this down.

Adversary

Satan' adversarial character is rooted in the belief of his superiority, feeling like he deserved equal reverence to God, a prideful conviction that he was worthy of the same honor and worship reserved for God alone. Blinded by arrogance and corrupted by self-exaltation, because of this, he saw God's character as a distortion and used this twisted perception as fuel for his ambition and rebellion.

This delusion did not remain in heaven. And with the same subtle deception, he used it to tempt Eve. The idea that God's character was distorted meant that His plans were also distorted. He carried this same delusion into the Garden of Eden, and it's recognizable in her temptation.

Let's look at the words spoken to Eve.

> Now the serpent was more subtil than any beast of the field which the LORD God had made. And he said unto the woman, Yea, hath God said, Ye shall not eat of

> every tree of the garden? And the woman said unto the serpent, We may eat of the fruit of the trees of the garden: But of the fruit of the tree which is in the midst of the garden, God hath said, Ye shall not eat of it, neither shall ye touch it, lest ye die<u>. And the serpent said unto the woman, Ye shall not surely die: For God doth know that in the day ye eat thereof, then your eyes shall be opened, and ye shall be as gods, knowing good and evil.</u> Genesis 3:1-5

Satan's response to Eve was a contradiction of the words spoken by God in Genesis 2:17 that says, *"But of the tree of the knowledge of good and evil, thou shalt not eat of it: for in the day that thou eatest thereof thou shalt surely die.* He caused her to believe that God was withholding something greater from her and that something could make her be like God.

These words proved Satan's confirmation bias, revealing his feelings of limitation compared to the Glory of almighty God. Any command given by God would not align with his belief; therefore, it must be interpreted in a way that proves to be unfair, thus the saying...*(quote)* *"And the serpent said unto the woman, Ye shall not surely die: For God doth know that in the day ye eat thereof, then your eyes shall be opened, and ye shall be as gods, knowing good and evil. " (unquote).* His belief projected "negative intentions" on God's part concerning his creations, showing that he is "not a loving and supreme God, because he is holding something back from you... "The power to be like Him". This was and is Satan's unfulfilled desire.

Not accepting or acknowledging his fault for his discontent, he blamed God in his mind for being unfair and restrictive. Again, look at what he said to Eve. The blame allowed him to avoid the discomfort of acknowledging his sinful nature and provided an avenue to blame God. He was and is the victim, driven now by a profound emptiness of empathy for God's divine order of things, only prioritizing his vengeful agenda.

Accuser

Satan's accusations of God, in his mind, help us to draw on the reason why he is called an accuser. The thing about an accuser is that they perceive, interpret, and magnify "flaws in others" while ignoring and/or not acknowledging their "own" flaws. Satan, as an accuser, cannot accept any form of good or righteousness that has the God of the bible attached to it. He cannot help but zero in on mistakes, weaknesses, and the sins of God's followers because His plan through Christ is the power that brings salvation and eternal life to all mankind. And anyone who accepts that plan and attempts to live by it is an enemy and a target aligned in his crosshairs.

> And I heard a loud voice saying in heaven, Now is come salvation, and strength, and the kingdom of our God, and the power of his Christ: for the accuser of our brethren is cast down, which accused them before our God day and night. – Revelation 12:10

Every failure in the life of the believer is used as an accusation or interpreted as definitive proof of guilt. He uses the believer's weaknesses, mistakes, and sins as evidence to support his belief that mankind deserves condemnation and should not be redeemed.

He selfishly projects his flaws and imperfections on us all with malicious and sinister intent. When one yields, he immediately rushes to make the case against the tempted. He paints the idea that God's creation is severely flawed and that no one can abide by the righteous laws that he set for mankind to live.

Let's look at Job.

> There was a man in the land of Uz, whose name was Job; and that man was perfect and upright, and one that feared God, and eschewed evil. And there were born unto him seven sons and three daughters. His substance also was seven thousand sheep, and three thousand camels, and five hundred yoke of oxen, and

> five hundred she asses, and a very great household; so that this man was the greatest of all the men of the east. And his sons went and feasted in their houses, every one his day; and sent and called for their three sisters to eat and to drink with them. And it was so, when the days of their feasting were gone about, that Job sent and sanctified them, and rose up early in the morning, and offered burnt offerings according to the number of them all: for Job said, It may be that my sons have sinned, and cursed God in their hearts. Thus did Job continually. Now there was a day when the sons of God came to present themselves before the LORD, and Satan came also among them. And the LORD said unto Satan, Whence comest thou? Then Satan answered the LORD, and said, From going to and fro in the earth, and from walking up and down in it. And the LORD said unto Satan, Hast thou considered my servant Job, that there is none like him in the earth, a perfect and an upright man, one that feareth God, and escheweth evil? Then Satan answered the LORD, and said, Doth Job fear God for nought? Hast not thou made an hedge about him, and about his house, and about all that he hath on every side? thou hast blessed the work of his hands, and his substance is increased in the land. But put forth thine hand now, and touch all that he hath, and he will curse thee to thy face. Genesis 1:1-11

Job was a man who not only was righteous in conduct, but was deeply reverent towards God. Job was a man who interceded for his children constantly, not wanting the elements of sin to enter their lives, yet despite all the integrity he displayed, Satan accused him before God. Job's righteousness placed him in Satan's crosshairs. His accusation against Job was that he was an upright man and one who shunned evil only because God had blessed him. The accusation was that his life was only "transactional". Satan challenged God with the claim that if He stripped him of his prosperity, Job would curse Him to His face.

Satan asserts in the story of Job that no human can genuinely serve God unless there is a reward involved. This accusation sits at the core of Satan's delusional framework. He works day and night fighting to distort the truth of God's relationship with man. Understand that this accusation was "not only personal," it is cosmic—a challenge to prove that faith itself is artificial.

Liar

Lucifer is the embodiment of "grandiose delusion" and no longer views himself as a creation of God, but as a unique, superior rival. With an unrealistic self-image and an inflated sense of entitlement, he believed he should have the position of power and authority over His creation. Remember his words, "to be like the Most High" *(Isaiah 14:12-14) and exalt his throne above God's.*

His delusion led him to believe that he could offer something better. If his ideas are better, then the truth of God's words must be proven wrong, so he has to "reframe God's truth with the intent to make God a liar. He is instrumental in this process because it involves unique concepts that make him a liar.

He doesn't simply speak falsehoods—he manufactures false realities. His lies are layered in half-truths, designed not only to mislead but to redefine what is true subtly. From the beginning, he has operated through a strategy of strategic contradiction. Satan lies not only by what he says but by what he implies—that God cannot be trusted, that His Word is flawed, and that His love is conditional. These insinuations form the foundation of his delusion and the root of his rebellion.

> He was a murderer from the beginning, and abode not in the truth, because there is no truth in him. When he speaketh a lie, he speaketh of his own: for he is a liar, and the father of it. St. John 8:44

Deception

For Satan to make God a liar, he has to manipulate God's truth by blending it with lies, subtly reinterpreting the truth, misapplying them, and making His words seem nonsensical and harsh, creating a counterfeit reality. This reality is one without God and His law. It involves these ideas and beliefs:

- You don't need God. You are sufficient and can create your reality and truth.
- Human reason and achievement are elevated above God's truth.
- All roads lead to heaven regardless of the faith you adopt, even if it's your own.

This deception is Satan's own "grandiose delusion" projected into the mind of the unbeliever. It is not the unbelievers' "personal truth". Its adopted into his mind because he rejects the gospel truth. And upon that rejection, the mind of the unbeliever is then "blinded".

> But if our gospel be hid, it is hid to them that are lost: In whom the god of this world hath blinded the minds of them which believe not, lest the light of the glorious gospel of Christ, who is the image of God, should shine unto them. – 2 Corinthians 4:3-4

Distortion

Moral standards have to be inverted by making what's truly sinful, appealing, liberating, and pleasing. Ungodly behavior is normalized:

- Glorifying violence, cruelty, or exploitation as strength or necessity
- Reframing dishonesty or corruption as pragmatism or cleverness
- Celebrating destructive behaviors as liberation or authenticity

Whereas Godly behavior is deemed as:

- Too restrictive or judgmental, resulting in attacks against those who speak truth and expose corruption, accusing them of being troublemakers.
- Condemning acts of genuine compassion, justice, or mercy as weakness or foolishness.
- Dismissing virtuous behavior as naive or self-serving

The end goal of distorting God's truth is that it fundamentally restructures the moral framework that allows people to distinguish between what is right and wrong. When societies or individuals lose the ability to differentiate between good and evil, they become vulnerable to accepting or even embracing genuinely harmful ideologies and behaviors. Obedience is viewed as bondage, and sin as freedom; worldly ideologies are embraced as spiritual enlightenment.

> Woe unto them that call evil good, and good evil; that put darkness for light, and light for darkness; that put bitter for sweet, and sweet for bitter! – Isaiah 5:20

Tempter

Satan appeals to the pride, fears, and desires of humanity by projecting his desires on those who are spiritually vulnerable. This projection is done through "enticements". He uses the same idea of "self-deification" that he had for himself to reel people into the false belief that they can define their own truth, morality, and destiny apart from God.

This is precisely what he did to Eve in the garden. He offered her autonomy disguised as "spiritual growth" by exploiting her emotional and doctrinal weakness. He distorted the divine truth of God and made it appear as a wise choice. Once Satan's word seeded her mind, temptation came and lured her into sin.

> And the serpent said unto the woman, Ye shall not surely die: For God doth know that in the day ye eat thereof, then your eyes shall be opened, and ye shall be as gods, knowing good and evil. And when the woman saw that the tree was good for food, and that it was pleasant to the eyes, and a tree to be desired to make one wise, she took of the fruit thereof, and did eat, and gave also unto her husband with her; and he did eat. Genesis 3:4-6

Everything about Satan serves two purposes: to serve himself and diminish the authority and character of God, making Him appear as a liar, imperfect, and conditional. He projects his deception onto humanity, enticing them to adopt his delusion and reject the truth. This is the essence of the strong delusion—a lie so compelling, it feels like truth to those who are spiritually unanchored.

CHAPTER FIVE

THE DEMONIC ROLE IN DELUSION

In 1 Kings 22:22, we find that God permitted a spirit (demon) to go down and be a lying spirit in the mouths of King Ahab's prophets. The reason for this was that Ahab constantly rejected the word of the Lord that was spoken by the prophet Micaiah. Remember, Ahab only wanted to hear what suited him.

In these dialogues, there are several significant factors that we must take note of to recognize that demons are not erratic and unintelligible beings focused solely on the destruction of mankind. They are highly intelligent, methodical, and hierarchical, strategically structured in a kingdom of darkness on a mission to oppose God's truth and manipulate mankind.

Understanding The Demonic

In many instances, when one thinks of a demon or possession, the idea that comes to mind is what is depicted in movies like The Exorcist. Head spinning, throwing up green vomit, objects flying across the room, and doors and windows opening and closing seemingly by themselves. This is Hollywood. Not reality. Demons are not mindless and chaotic. Demons operate by permission or as judgment, mainly through the mind and behavior of men. They motivate by thought and suggestion to encourage men to do things that are contrary to the word of God.

There are three characteristics that you must understand about demons. They are intelligent. They possess knowledge, reason, memory, and strategy.

> And in the synagogue there was a man, which had a spirit of an unclean devil, and cried out with a loud voice, Saying, Let us alone; what have we to do with thee, thou Jesus of Nazareth? art thou come to destroy us? I know thee who thou art; the Holy One of God.- St. Luke 4:33–34

This demon recognized Jesus, understood His authority, and responded based on theological awareness. Intelligence is required to reason, plan, deceive, and fear judgment, which demons clearly exhibit.

They have emotions. Demons feel fear, rage, and torment. They tremble at God's authority and are terrified of judgment.

> Thou believest that there is one God; thou doest well: the devils also believe, and tremble. - James 2:19

> And, behold, they cried out, saying, What have we to do with thee, Jesus, thou Son of God? art thou come hither to torment us before the time? - Matthew 8:29

Their emotion of fear is linked to knowledge of their coming judgment. They feel torment and dread at the presence of Christ and His truth.

They possess a will. Demons make decisions. They ask permission. They choose targets. They express desires and intentions.

> When the unclean spirit is gone out of a man, he walketh through dry places, seeking rest, and findeth none. Then he saith, I will return into my house from whence I came out...
> Matthew 12:43–44

The scripture proves that they demonstrate self-awareness, effective decision-making, and a clear purpose. Demons have plans, and those plans are typically aimed at re-entry, oppression, and ultimate destruction. And the most effective key they use is unbelief. The doorway of delusion.

The Rulers of The Darkness

In the hierarchy of Satan's demonic kingdom, there are positions of power, influence, and government that consist of principalities, which are the regional spirits that hold territorial assignments. Then there are the powers that are the governing spirits that manipulate laws and systems. But the workers who carry out these assignments are called the "rulers of the darkness". These spirits or demons are "specifically tasked with "KEEPING HUMANITY BLIND FROM THE SPIRITUAL TRUTH." As a result, "spiritual wickedness", depravity, moral badness is plotted and carried throughout the whole of mankind's minds, "the high places" and into society.

> For we wrestle not against flesh and blood, but against principalities, against powers, against the rulers of the darkness of this world, against spiritual wickedness in high places. – Ephesians

"Rulers" serve higher powers as agents sent to carry out the task or assignments relating to the laws of "principalities" assigned to territories. In the case of demons, these laws contradict the laws of God. How they do this is found in the term "darkness". It comes from the Greek term *"skotos"*, which means "darkness or obscurity," often relating to moral terms or spiritual terms. It is the absence of light, knowledge, and wisdom —a spiritual condition that keeps mankind in sin, ignorance, and bondage, resulting in a life lived without the truth of God's word.

A mind disconnected from God becomes the "high place" where Satan rules and demons operate by causing the person(s) to carry out wicked acts. In 1st Kings 22, the evil spirit was allowed to enter and "possess the prophets to speak lies". Because Ahab refused to accept the truth, the spirit in the mouth of the prophets "perverted the truth.", enforcing the lie that Ahab wanted to believe.

"Men loved darkness rather than light, because their deeds were evil." -John 3:19

Demons or rulers of the darkness are messengers of deception, whose purpose is to influence people through false doctrine, compromised theology, and carnal reasoning. They twist scripture, mixing truth with error by promoting prosperity without repentance and grace without obedience. They promote emotionalism over bible doctrine. Many are now claiming to be led by God in ways that contradict Scripture, prioritizing praise, worship, and emotional experience over solid Bible teaching, and chasing after experiences rather than holiness. These messengers are deluding minds, causing spiritual immaturity and a culture where feelings validate truth over God's word.

For the time will come when they will not endure sound doctrine; but after their own lusts shall they heap to themselves teachers, having itching ears." - 2 Timothy 4:3

Chapter Six

The Demonization of Social Media

Demons are strategic communicators, not just spiritual oppressors. They influence culture by speaking through people, especially those in *religious authority who have become* corrupted, prideful, or seduced by fame and power. In this age, their most effective weapons are not only the occult, but also the camera, microphone, and algorithm.

> Now the Spirit speaketh expressly, that in the latter times some shall depart from the faith, giving heed to <u>seducing spirits, and doctrines of devils;</u> Speaking lies in hypocrisy; having their conscience seared with a hot iron; - 1 Timothy 4:1-2

One of Satan's new sanctuaries is the digital pulpit. Platforms like TikTok, Instagram, and Facebook enable demons through podcasters and influencers to gain mass influence without accountability, pastoral oversight, and spiritual power in the lord, which results in spiritual immaturity and failure. These platforms allow false prophets and teachers to elevate voices that normalize sin under the banner of grace, amplify heretical trends that contradict the word of God, and spread deception through the prophetic that feeds self-worship.

If a person believes a doctrine or idea that contradicts the word of God, demons actively enforce that belief, not just through temptation, but also by working through the mouths of teachers who have departed from sound doctrine or by adopting ideas from motivational influencers who teach doctrines of humanism, spiritualism, or self-deification.

Delusion is not just believing a lie, it's being convinced that the lie is the truth. When the word of God is rejected by the hearer, due to that word contradicting their lifestyle, they immediately become "spiritually vulnerable". This vulnerability becomes the "doorway" for demons to enforce a "belief system" that's comfortable, emotionally appealing, self-exalting and biblically hollow.

False Prophets with Followers, Not Fruit

The digital landscape has witnessed an alarming proliferation of false prophets, whose influence extends far beyond the mere dissemination of erroneous teachings. Their rise is linked to the audience they cultivate and the desires they exploit.

The Apostle Paul, warned of such a time, declaring,

> For the time will come when they will not endure sound doctrine; but after their own lusts shall they heap to themselves teachers, having itching ears - 2 Timothy 4:3.

This powerful passage underscores a critical shift in spiritual appetite: a departure from a hunger for gospel truth towards a craving for messages that caters to personal desires and preconceived notions, rather than challenging them. "Itching ears" are not genuinely seeking divine truth or transformative wisdom. Their spiritual inclination is driven by a deep-seated desire for confirmation of existing biases, a craving for personal empowerment that sidesteps genuine humility, and an insatiable need for emotional validation—even when such validation directly contradicts the Word of God.

These individuals become fertile ground for deception, willingly embracing narratives that soothe their discomfort, inflate their self-perception, or justify their unrighteous desires, regardless of how far removed these narratives are from biblical sound doctrine. This selective hearing creates a dangerous echo chamber, where the pursuit of truth is supplanted by the pursuit of self-gratification.

It is precisely within this fertile ground of "itching ears" that demonic forces operate with chilling effectiveness. Their work is not limited to simply inspiring the teaching of outright lies; it thrives more potently in cultivating the *desire* for those lies within the hearts of listeners. These digital voices, amplified by platforms and algorithms, can subtly or overtly become idols in the lives of their followers. The charisma of the personality, the slick production, or the promise of an easy spiritual path can elevate these teachers to an unholy pedestal, transforming their pronouncements into "doctrines of devils" (1 Timothy 4:1). The very intimacy offered by a camera lens can tragically morph into a false sanctuary, where comfort is found in deception rather than in the authentic presence of God.

Social Media and Demonic Doorways

Beliefs act as crucial entry points into the human mind, and when these beliefs are rooted in falsehood, they become formidable enforcers of delusion. There is doctrine that does not originate from divine revelation but springs forth from the corrupted impulses of human nature. This doctrine is packaged in alluring affirmations like…

- You are enough.
- trust your truth.

- manifest your destiny.

...and subtly promotes a dangerous form of self-deification. These are not novel concepts of modern spirituality; rather, they are ancient, seductive lies, direct echoes of the very whisper that first deceived Eve in the Garden of Eden...

Ye shall be as gods... Genesis 3:5

This lie promised autonomy, divine knowledge, and self-sufficiency apart from God, while appealing to humanity's desire for independence and ultimate control. The enemy's strategy remains chillingly consistent; only the methods of propagation *have been adapted for the digital age* through social media platforms.

Tragically, in an act of divine judgment, demons continue to articulate these words of rebellion and self-exaltation through the very influencers who have embraced these delusions. The reels, livestreams, and podcast microphones become their pulpits, broadcasting a deceptive gospel that caters directly to the fallen human desire for self-worship. The very platforms intended for connection become conduits for judgment, solidifying a delusional framework where personal feelings and desires usurp divine truth, ultimately leading both the deceived influencers and their unsuspecting followers further into the spiritual bondage of delusion.

Chapter Seven

Delusion and The Demonization of the Mind.

Demonization does not begin with possession. It begins with "persuasion". They target the mind with evil intent to reshape beliefs, influence thinking and ultimately distort one's perception of reality. A person who lives in a distorted reality suffers from a spiritual hardening of the mind. Correction is seen as "oppression". Truth is heard and seen as "hate". Sin becomes celebrated and deception in the case of the religious is seen as divine revelation and prophetic. Their moral compass is no longer controlled or allowed to be controlled by God, but is only driven by emotions, one's own desires and cultural norms.

But remember to get to get this state, you must reject the truth. This is the whole goal of demons. You must choose comfort over conviction and choose the error over the truth of God's word. Why? The rejection of the truth is the key that opens the doorway to your mind for them to enter. Willful unbelief provides demons legal access to your mind where they will corrupt your intelligence with lies until it becomes part of your identity.

The danger that lurks in the darkness of this demonic strategy is the formation of a reprobate mind. a mind that has been so corrupted by persistent unbelief and lies that it no longer discerns between right and wrong, good and evil, truth and deception.

> And even as they did not like to retain God in their knowledge, God gave them over to a reprobate mind. Romans 1:28

The Psychology of the Reprobate Mind

A "reprobate mind" is a mind that has been examined and tested by the standards of the word of God and has been found "unfit" to retain its truth. The consequence of being judged as a reprobate comes about through "persistent and deliberate rejection" hence the scripture, *"they did not like to retain..."* Through a prolonged rejection of the word, rebellion becomes the norm and the soil for deceptive thought spreads and grows deeper.

From a psychological viewpoint, a reprobate mind is classified as pathological cognitive distortion—a deep-seated inability to recognize or submit to objective reality. The DSM-5 outlines features common in antisocial and narcissistic personality disorders, such as chronic defiance of moral norms, lack of empathy, and manipulative thinking. In simple terms the conscience of the individual becomes "seared" where the moral sensitivity which provokes conviction of sin becomes numb "beyond recognition".

> Speaking lies in hypocrisy; having their conscience seared with a hot iron; 1 Timothy 4:2

The reprobated person not only resists correction but becomes more emboldened in sin interpreting their condition as freedom rather than bondage. Moral boundaries are blurred and then destroyed, being "authentic" or "true to oneself" is deemed as a justification of sin, rebellion is celebrated and glorified.

> But evil men and seducers shall wax worse and worse, deceiving, and being deceived. - 2 Timothy 3:13

Demons play a central role in cultivating this condition. Once truth is willfully rejected, the mind becomes spiritually unguarded, providing demons with the legal right to build ideological strongholds that reinforce the individuals twisted worldview and burying it deeper and deeper into the psyche, making it more and more difficult for them to break free from their distorted worldview.

This distorted worldview, being reinforced by the demonic through deception and pride escalates to delusion, making the mind a sanctuary for demonic influence converting the individual to become an agent of deception, further spreading the lies to others.

Demons and Strongholds

> … to the pulling down of strong holds;) Casting down imaginations, and every high thing that exalteth itself against the knowledge of God, and bringing into captivity every thought to the obedience of Christ; - 2 Corinthians 10:4-5

A stronghold signifies a fortified mindset, a mental fortress constructed to resist God's truth. When an individual encounters a lie—perhaps something seemingly minor like "God cannot forgive me" or "I define my own truth." If this lie is embraced rather than rejected, it takes root, most likely being fueled and driven by some emotion, trauma, or pride, the agreement with the lie becomes entrenched in the mind to the point where the lie feels like part of the person's identity. Finally, demons gain a foothold in this mental space and reinforce the stronghold, using temptation, deception, and accusation to keep it in place.

Demons through the process of repetition will cultivate the agreement with the lie and then guard the resulting belief system. This is how delusion grows—the individual cannot distinguish error from truth because the stronghold has become a lens through which all reality is interpreted. As an example, a stronghold of sexual immorality can start with exposure to pornography (the lie that lust is harmless), is then reinforced by culture ("everyone does it"), and eventually it transforms into an identity ("this is who I am").

Another well-known example would be gender confusion. A 2022 Gallup Poll revealed a significant shift: over 21% of Gen Z now identify as LGBTQ+, a dramatic increase compared to older generations. While numerous factors contribute to this trend, some sociologists propose that *social contagion and algorithmic reinforcement*, particularly from platforms like TikTok, are instrumental. They suggest these digital influences shape identity based on *affirmation rather than objective reality*.

> <u>Professing themselves to be wise, they became fools</u> And changed the glory of the uncorruptible God into an image made like to corruptible man, and to birds, and fourfooted beasts, and creeping things. Wherefore God also gave them up to uncleanness through the lusts of their own hearts, to dishonour their own bodies between themselves: Who changed the truth of God into a lie, and worshipped and served the creature more than the Creator, who is blessed for ever. Amen. For this cause God gave them up unto vile affections: for even

> their women did change the natural use into that which is against nature: And likewise also the men, leaving the natural use of the woman, burned in their lust one toward another; men with men working that which is unseemly, and receiving in themselves that recompence of their error which was meet. Romans 1:22-27

Imaginations and High Things

The false affirmations of belief that shape the identity are made up of two types of thought. Imaginations and high things that exalts itself above the knowledge of God. These two categories are not just abstract ideas - they represent the architecture of spiritual influence in deception. They are part of the leading cause of departing from Gods divine framework of thinking that can result in distorted understandings of truth, identities that reject God as Creator and leading to profound confusion.

Imaginations

Imaginations can be viewed as "reasonings" that involve self-reliance and pride and subtle influence of spiritual darkness. At their core, imaginations are mental constructs that elevate personal desires, feelings, and cultural norms above the authority of God. From a psychological perspective, these imaginations mirror cognitive distortions which are faulty patterns of thinking that warp a person's understanding of reality.

For example, *catastrophizing* imagines the worst outcome ("If I surrender to God, everything will collapse"), while *emotional reasoning* insists that feelings define truth ("I feel like woman trapped in a man's body, so I must be a man. I feel worthless; therefore, I am worthless). These distortions create fertile soil for demonic deception because they condition the mind to reject objective truth in favor of a subjective experience.

According to Barna Research, only 6% of Americans maintain a biblical worldview, while most believe that "looking within" is the best way to find truth—an approach that aligns perfectly with Satan's original deception in Genesis 3:5: *"Ye shall be as gods."*

Ungodly imaginations construct false identities, driving us toward sensuality, materialism, and emotional gratification. This trend aligns with a significant cultural shift: Gallup data reveals that 7.1% of U.S. adults now identify as LGBTQ+, a figure that has doubled in just a decade. This rise coincides with the increasing acceptance of moral relativism and identity based on feelings. Theologically, these examples point to vain imaginations and empty ways of thinking that cloud our understanding of God's character and distort His intended design for humanity.

Demons strategically exploit these imaginations. They introduce lies, reinforce them through cultural repetition and personal experience, and then encourage agreement. Once the individual consents to the lie, whether about God, themselves, or morality, demons gain legal ground to fortify the deception thus creating a stronghold. Over time, lies become indistinguishable from identity: deception feels like freedom, and truth feels like oppression.

Arguments and High Things

Imaginations or reasonings work together with "arguments" which are the "defenses of error formed by reasonings." They are the mental justifications and intellectual frameworks designed to dismiss Gods truth. The Greek word for *arguments* is often translated from the same root as *logismos* meaning calculations, reasonings, or arguments, but here, it emphasizes a systematic and entrenched form of opposition. While imaginations may begin as fleeting rationalizations or emotions, arguments are established belief systems *that harden the mind against repentance.* They are the ideological fortresses that feel intellectually satisfying and emotionally reassuring but are fundamentally hostile to divine authority.

Barna's Research studies reveal that 88% of Americans believe the key to fulfillment is to "look within," reinforcing the argument that personal desire is the ultimate moral authority. These arguments then become powerful barriers to conviction: instead of acknowledging sin, people rebrand rebellion *as authenticity or enlightenment.*

Theologically, arguments are the spiritual strongholds that demons actively build and protect. This is why Paul warns that these belief systems "exalt themselves against the knowledge of God." They are not neutral; they are in competition with God's Word for authority over the heart and mind. For example,

- The argument of religious pluralism (*"All paths lead to God"*) directly contradicts Jesus' exclusive claim in John 14:6: *"I am the way, the truth, and the life: no man cometh unto the Father, but by me*
- The argument of moral relativism (*"What's true for you isn't true for me"*) defies the objective standards of God's law
- The argument of religious pantheism (Pantheism (*God is everything and everyone).*

- The argument of Neo-Paganism / Ancestral Veneration ("You don't need the Bible; your ancestors will guide you.")

When a person continues to agree with these arguments, they do not simply remain deceived, they become increasingly hardened, until God eventually gives them over to a reprobate mind as judgment (Romans 1:28). This is why confronting arguments is essential: they are not just intellectual opinions; they are spiritual fortresses that keep people enslaved to darkness and resistant to salvation.

Chapter Eight

The Falling Away and The Mystery Of Iniquity

The prophecy of a great Falling Away is more than a prediction of decline; it is the revelation of how delusion takes hold of a generation that refuses the truth. The Apostle Paul warns with unmistakable clarity that *"that day shall not come, except there come a falling away first"* (2 Thessalonians 2:3). The Greek term *apostasia* means not merely drifting into error but revolting against the authority of God Himself. This deliberate abandonment of sound doctrine opens the door to spiritual deception so pervasive that it prepares the hearts of many for the ultimate counterfeit: the rise of the man of sin

The Falling Away

At its core, the falling away is the gateway to delusion. It begins when professing believers willingly exchange the unchanging standard of Scripture for teachings that soothe their consciences and indulge their desires. Paul foresaw a time when many would *"not endure sound doctrine"* and instead would *"heap to themselves teachers, having itching ears"* (2 Timothy 4:3). This is not merely doctrinal drift—it is a willful embrace of error that feels comforting precisely because it requires no sacrifice and demands no repentance.

When people persist in rejecting the truth, they do not remain spiritually neutral; they become vulnerable to deception so persuasive that it eventually feels indistinguishable from truth itself. This is how delusion begins: as a preference for pleasing lies over uncomfortable reality.

One of the clearest marks that delusion is taking root is the normalization of sin and the rebranding of rebellion as authenticity. Jesus declared that in the last days, *"because iniquity shall abound, the love of many shall wax cold"* (Matthew 24:12). This moral compromise paves the way for spiritual blindness. Where conviction once produced repentance, now it provokes hostility. Where truth once set people free, it is dismissed as intolerant or outdated.

Hyper-grace doctrines teach that sin is no obstacle to fellowship with God, while universalism denies the exclusivity of Christ's atonement altogether. These deceptions flourish because they offer a religion that never confronts sin—a belief system where delusion can grow unchecked. In this environment, people not only tolerate error but defend it fiercely, believing the lie that God is unconcerned with holiness. As Paul wrote, *"Who changed the truth of God into a lie..."* (Romans 1:25).

This process is neither new nor unforeseen; Scripture records its pattern repeatedly. In the Old Testament, Israel abandoned the covenant and embraced worthless idols, provoking

God to declare, *"They have forsaken me the fountain of living waters..."* (Jeremiah 2:13). In the early church, Hymenaeus and Philetus spread teachings that corroded faith in the resurrection (2 Timothy 2:17–18), while Demas deserted Paul out of love for the present world (2 Timothy 4:10). But in the last days, this cycle will escalate into a worldwide apostasy.

The falling away becomes the fertile soil in which the final delusion matures into a delusion so strongly that those who reject truth will be given over to believe the lie (2 Thessalonians 2:11). This is the most sobering reality of all: persistent rebellion does not merely lead to confusion; it leads to divinely permitted delusion that darkens the mind and hardens the heart.

The Mystery of Iniquity

While the falling Away represents the visible, outward abandonment of truth, the Mystery of Iniquity describes the hidden spiritual mechanism that drives that rebellion. The Apostle Paul declared, *"For the mystery of iniquity doth already work..."* (2 Thessalonians 2:7). This phrase reveals a profound insight: long before the Antichrist is revealed, a concealed system of lawlessness is already at work in the world, undermining biblical faith, corrupting human conscience, and preparing minds to embrace ultimate deception.

The word *mystery* means something previously hidden that is now being disclosed. Iniquity (ἀνομία, *anomia*) is not merely the presence of sin but the spirit of lawlessness—a defiant refusal to acknowledge God's authority. This Mystery of Iniquity operates quietly, often unnoticed by those who are not discerning. It does not announce itself with obvious evil but cloaks itself in plausible philosophies and attractive spiritual counterfeits. It fuels the ideologies that call good evil and evil good, producing the cultural confusion we see today.

> "evil men and seducers shall wax worse and worse, deceiving, and being deceived" - 2 Timothy 3:13.

This dynamic is why so many who once professed truth can drift into delusion without recognizing the shift. What begins as compromise becomes corruption, and what seems like harmless openness to new ideas becomes a hardened resistance to truth. As the restraining influence of God's Spirit is increasingly withdrawn, lawlessness gains momentum, culminating in the appearance of the man of sin.

Perhaps the most sobering aspect of the Mystery of Iniquity is that it does not merely deceive individuals, it reshapes entire cultures and institutions. It is the spirit behind movements that dismiss Scripture as irrelevant, redefine morality according to popular opinion, and celebrate rebellion as enlightenment. It operates through religious pluralism that denies the exclusivity of Christ and through progressive ideologies that exalt self as the ultimate authority.

In this way, the Mystery of Iniquity not only prepares the world to embrace Antichrist but also blinds it to the judgment that inevitably follows. Those who reject the truth do not remain neutral; they are swept into a process of deception that God eventually confirms as judgment: *"God shall send them strong delusion, that they should believe a lie"* (2 Thessalonians 2:11). This is why discernment and unwavering commitment to God's Word have never been more vital. To resist the Mystery of Iniquity, one must love the truth more than comfort, popularity, or personal opinion.

Key Indicators of The Falling Away

One of the clearest indicators that the Mystery of Iniquity is advancing in our generation is the dramatic erosion of a biblical worldview in society at large. According to Barna's 2020 research, only 6% of Americans now hold a biblical worldview, while a staggering 88% affirm self-defined morality—the idea that individuals have the right to determine right and wrong for themselves.

This is precisely the lawlessness that Scripture warns will characterize the end times, when *"every man did that which was right in his own eyes"* (Judges 21:25). The normalization of self-exaltation, relativism, and moral confusion is not random social drift—it is the coordinated outworking of an unseen system of iniquity designed to harden hearts against truth. In this cultural climate, the absolutes of God's Word are increasingly viewed as oppressive, intolerant, or irrelevant, laying the groundwork for delusion to spread unchecked.

Church Apostasy

The same trend is unmistakable in the visible church, where the Falling Away has begun to shape teaching, worship, and community life. Gallup's 2022 report revealed that church membership in the United States dropped below 50% for the first time in recorded history. Even among those who still attend, many no longer expect to be confronted with the demands of holiness or the urgency of repentance.

Instead, sermons are increasingly shaped by popular psychology, self-help principles, and prosperity promises rather than the convicting message of the cross. This shift fulfills Paul's warning that in the last days, people would *"not endure sound doctrine"*. The Mystery of Iniquity works subtly within the church to redefine Christianity into a faith that comforts the flesh rather than crucifies it, and this redefinition is one of the greatest betrayals of our time.

Personal Apostasy

At the individual level, the rise of spiritual indifference is perhaps the most sobering sign of all. Pew Research has shown that 26% of American adults now identify as religious "Nones," a figure that has grown rapidly in just a few decades. Yet many of these same individuals still describe themselves as "spiritual," revealing how the Mystery of Iniquity entices people to embrace a counterfeit form of faith that requires no submission to God.

This is the perfect breeding ground for delusion: a spirituality that feels authentic but denies the power of truth. As Jesus warned,

> "…because iniquity shall abound, the love of many shall wax cold" - Matthew 24:12.

The infrastructure of apostasy is not merely being constructed around us—it is being built within minds that once knew conviction but have been traded for autonomy. In this hour, the call to discernment, faithfulness, and unwavering commitment to Scripture is more urgent than ever.

Chapter Nine

The Word Made Flesh

> In the beginning was the Word, and the Word was with God, and the Word was God. The same was in the beginning with God. All things were made by him; and without him was not any thing made that was made… And the Word was made flesh, and dwelt among us - John 1:1–3, 14

Scripture reveals that Jesus Christ is not merely a prophet or a moral teacher but the very embodiment of the eternal Word of God. The Greek term *Logos* goes far beyond the idea of spoken speech; it refers to the complete expression of God's thoughts, concepts, and reasoning. Jesus is the visible manifestation of the divine mind itself—the living revelation of how God thinks, feels, and purposes. In Him, the eternal nature of God stepped into time and space so that humanity could see, hear, and touch the truth in person.

Jesus, The Divine Mind of God Revealed

This same reality is echoed in Hebrews, where we read that in former times, God spoke through prophets in many different ways, but *"hath in these last days spoken unto us by his Son… who being the brightness of his glory, and the express image of his person"* (Hebrews 1:1–3). The Greek word translated *"express image"* means the exact imprint or precise representation of something. It emphasizes that Jesus is not a partial reflection but the perfect imprint of the invisible God's nature and thoughts. To see Jesus is to see God's character made visible. This means the revelation of Christ is not merely informational—it is transformational, because in encountering Him, we encounter the fullness of God's mind and heart toward us.

Colossians further affirms that Christ is *"the image of the invisible God"* and the one through whom all things were created (Colossians 1:15–17). Jesus Christ alone reveals the complete truth of who God is to humanity. He is not simply a mirror but the substance—the one in whom divine thoughts and intentions take on visible form.

In a world filled with speculation about God's nature, Jesus stands as the unchanging standard by which every idea about God must be measured. When the Word became flesh, truth itself entered the human story, and it is this truth that Satan and his kingdom most violently oppose. To reject Jesus is to reject the very mind of God—and it is this rejection that ultimately opens the door to delusion.

Jesus, The Thoughts and Ways of God

> "For my thoughts are not your thoughts, neither are your ways my ways, saith the LORD." – Isaiah 55:8

In this single sentence, God reveals that His intentions, designs, and methods are infinitely higher and holier than anything humanity can imagine. The Hebrew words used here—*machăshābâh* for "thoughts," meaning the purposeful weaving of plans, and *derek* for "ways," meaning a chosen path—emphasize that apart from revelation, we cannot even begin to grasp God's mind or understand how He works. This gulf between divine wisdom and human perception is precisely why humanity has stumbled in darkness, straying into error, idolatry, and self-made religion. Without a bridge between God's transcendent thoughts and our finite understanding, we remain bound to confusion and spiritual blindness.

This is why the coming of Jesus Christ is so staggering in its significance: He is not merely a prophet explaining God's ways, He is the perfect manifestation of those thoughts and ways in human flesh. As John 1:1 and 1:14 declare, *"In the beginning was the Word... and the Word was made flesh, and dwelt among us."*

The Greek word *Logos* means much more than a spoken word; it is the full expression of divine reasoning and intention.

Hebrews 1:3 reinforces this reality by calling Jesus *"the express image of his person,"* the exact imprint of God's nature. When Christ walked the earth, He demonstrated exactly what God thinks about sin, holiness, mercy, and redemption. Every action and every word was a revelation of the mind of God toward humanity—no longer hidden behind mystery but living and visible in the person of the Son.

Because Jesus is the thoughts and ways of God incarnate, all truth finds its fulfillment and definition in Him. This is why Satan wages relentless war against the revelation of Christ, blinding minds and hardening hearts through deception and delusion.

"the god of this world hath blinded the minds of them which believe not, lest the light of the glorious gospel of Christ… should shine unto them. - 2 Corinthians 4:4

The conflict is not simply over doctrines or religious systems; it is a cosmic struggle over whether humanity will see and embrace the One who embodies God's perfect thoughts and saving ways. Delusion flourishes where Jesus is misunderstood, diminished, or rejected, because to reject Him is to reject the very mind and heart of God. In a world of counterfeit wisdom and self-defined truth, the person of Christ stands as the unchanging revelation of God's eternal purposes, calling every generation back to Himself.

Satan, The Father of Lies

From the opening chapters of Genesis, Scripture reveals that Satan's nature is defined by deception, making him the complete opposite of Jesus Christ. Jesus described Satan plainly in John 8:44, saying, *"He is a liar, and the father of it."* Where Christ is the Word made flesh, the perfect revelation of God's thoughts and truth—Satan is the originator of all falsehood.

The phrase "father of it" means he conceived and birthed every lie that has ever corrupted the human heart. His first tactic in the garden was to question God's Word, whispering, *"Hath God said?"* (Genesis 3:1). This subtle challenge to God's truth was the seed of all delusion, showing that the serpent's strategy has never changed: to distort what God has spoken so that humanity will doubt His character and reject His authority.

This opposition to Christ's truth is not limited to isolated lies, it is a perpetual counterfeit of everything God reveals. Where

Christ demonstrates the mind and heart of God, Satan deliberately corrupts that revelation with half-truths and spiritual counterfeits. Revelation 12:9 describes Satan as *"that old serpent... which deceiveth the whole world."* His scope is global, but his objective is singular: to obscure the identity and work of Christ so that the world remains blind to salvation.

Every false religion, every deceptive philosophy, every twisting of Scripture ultimately has one aim—to keep humanity from recognizing Jesus as the Word made flesh and the only way to the Father.

> I am the way, the truth, and the life: no man cometh unto the Father, but by me. – John 14:6

This is why the warfare over truth is a warfare over minds. As Paul wrote in 2 Corinthians 4:3–4, *"...the god of this world hath blinded the minds of them which believe not, lest the light of the glorious gospel of Christ... should shine unto them."* Demonic deception specifically targets the human mind because it is through understanding that people come to faith.

Satan blinds spiritual perception so that the gospel appears irrelevant, offensive, or foolish. He replaces truth with appealing distortions—lies that seem compassionate or progressive but subtly lead away from Christ. Over time, these deceptions harden the heart against conviction, making repentance feel unnecessary and truth feel oppressive.

Ultimately, this conflict is not about abstract ideas or moral debates—it is about a war against the person of Jesus Christ Himself. When Satan attacks truth, he is attacking Christ because Christ is the embodiment of all truth. This is why 2 Thessalonians 2:9–11 warns of a time when Satan will unleash a final wave of deception *"with all power and signs and lying wonders,"* culminating in a strong delusion sent by God as judgment upon those who rejected the truth. This delusion is not mere confusion—it is the consequence of resisting Christ until God allows deception to become an unbreakable prison.

In the end, every spiritual battle comes down to this: whether humanity will embrace the truth revealed in Jesus or yield to the father of lies. Jesus births truth in the hearts of those who receive Him, transforming minds and restoring sight. Satan, by contrast, births lies that blind, corrupt, and ultimately destroy.

This is why delusion is so dangerous, it is not simply believing a harmless error; it is siding with the one who has hated Christ from the beginning. The war for the soul is, at its core, a war over the revelation of who Jesus is. To love truth is to love Him;

to reject truth is to stand with the enemy whose only purpose is to keep the world in darkness.

CHAPTER TEN

ESCAPING THE JUDGMENT OF DELUSION

Yielding to the truth of the gospel and escaping the grip of delusion begins with a decisive commitment to love the truth above all else. Delusion does not take root simply because a person lacks information, it takes root when the heart prefers comforting lies over convicting reality. As Paul warned in 2 Thessalonians 2:10, those who perish do so "because they received not the love of the truth, that they might be saved." The first step is to ask God to soften your heart so you treasure His Word more than cultural trends, personal feelings, or the approval of others. This love for truth becomes the soil where transformation begins.

Yield To The Truth

From the posture of surrendered affection for truth, you must then test every thought and teaching against Scripture. Delusion thrives in unchecked imaginations and cognitive distortions that sound spiritual but contradict God's Word. Paul instructs believers to *"cast down imaginations, and every high thing that exalteth itself against the knowledge of God"* (2 Corinthians 10:5).

Every philosophy, religious idea, or personal conviction must be measured by the unchanging standard of the Bible. If a thought does not align with Scripture, it must be rejected no matter how persuasive or popular it seems. This habit trains the mind to recognize the difference between truth and deception.

At the same time, a life yielded to the gospel is marked by submission to the Lordship of Christ. Jesus declared, *"I am the way, the truth, and the life"* (John 14:6). To embrace truth is to embrace Him personally and fully. This means surrendering every area of life relating to your ambitions, your morality, and your identity to His authority. Transformation comes as you walk daily in repentance and humility, allowing His Spirit to renew your thinking (Romans 12:2).

Mind Transformation

> And be renewed in the spirit of your mind -
> Ephesians 4:23

Mind transformation and freedom from deception does not happen by accident. The Greek word for "renewed" (ἀνανεόω, *ananeóō*) means to be made new in quality, to be renovated, or to have a fresh way of thinking. This renewal is not merely spiritual. It involves the Holy Spirit illuminating the mind, exposing lies, and replacing them with truth. This is the divine antidote to delusion: when God's Word saturates the mind and the Spirit empowers the heart, deception loses its grip. Instead of being conformed to the shifting patterns of the world, believers are conformed to the unchanging truth of Christ. This is why Paul elsewhere urges, *"be not conformed to this world: but be ye transformed by the renewing of your mind"* (Romans 12:2). When the mind is renewed, it becomes a place where God's thoughts take root and grow.

This renewal is critical because delusion is, at its core, a corruption of the mind. As 2 Thessalonians 2 explains, those who do not love the truth are given over to strong delusion as a form of judgment. When people reject conviction and prefer comforting lies, their thinking becomes darkened, and eventually, their perception of reality is distorted beyond recognition. In this state, evil is called good, and good is called evil.

But Ephesians 4:23 shows the way out: the mind must be continually washed by the truth of Scripture and yielded to the Spirit's correction. This is not a one-time experience but a daily posture of humility, repentance, and openness to God's instruction. Just as the body needs daily nourishment, the mind needs daily renewal to resist the encroachment of deception.

Ultimately, being renewed in the spirit of your mind is how you align your thoughts with the mind of Christ. It is how you anchor your convictions in eternal truth rather than the shifting currents of culture. This renewal protects you from the judgment of delusion because it cultivates a love for what is true and a hatred for what is false. As your mind is made new, you become increasingly sensitive to error and increasingly anchored in the reality of who Jesus is, "the Word made flesh".

The Spirit uses the Word to expose every counterfeit and demolish every stronghold of deception. In this way, Ephesians 4:23 is not just an encouragement, it is a divine strategy for survival in a world where deception is rapidly becoming the norm.

Be Accountable to Oneself

One of the most important ways to remain sensitive to the truth of the gospel and guard against delusion is by committing to continual self-examination. The Apostle Paul commands believers with this intelligence:

> Examine yourselves, whether ye be in the faith; prove your own selves. - 2 Corinthians 13:5

This is a spiritual discipline. Regularly you must measure your attitudes, beliefs, and behaviors against the unchanging standard of God's Word. When you examine yourself honestly, you expose any seeds of compromise before they take root. This practice of self-accountability keeps your conscience tender, your convictions clear, and your faith authentic in a world that constantly tempts you to drift into self-deception.

Along with self-examination, Scripture calls every believer to renew the mind daily. Spiritual transformation is impossible without mental renewal. It requires a deliberate choice to reject the patterns and priorities of the age and instead fill your thoughts with God's truth. This daily discipline recalibrates your heart to love what He loves and hate what He hates. When your mind is saturated with Scripture, you develop discernment to recognize even subtle forms of deception. In this way, renewing your mind becomes a safeguard against the creeping influence of compromise that eventually leads to delusion.

Another essential part of avoiding spiritual blindness is cultivating a posture of humble receptivity to correction.

> Rebuke a wise man, and he will love thee. –
> Proverbs 9:8

Those who refuse correction harden their hearts and gradually lose their sensitivity to conviction. By contrast, the humble welcome godly rebuke, understanding it as a gift that keeps them from wandering. Accountability to yourself means you refuse to shield yourself from uncomfortable truth or surround yourself only with voices that affirm you. Instead, you invite trusted believers to speak candidly into your life. This humility protects you from the pride that blinds so many and becomes the fertile soil where repentance and growth can flourish.

> If we walk in the light, as he is in the light, we have fellowship one with another... 1 John 1:7

When you bring hidden struggles into the open before God and mature believers, you break the power of shame and secrecy, two of the enemy's most effective tools for nurturing delusion. Confession keeps your heart soft, your conscience clean, and your spirit responsive to the Holy Spirit's promptings. Rather than concealing compromise, you acknowledge it, repent of it, and invite God to cleanse you. This transparency dismantles the strongholds that thrive in darkness and anchors you in the "freedom of the truth".

CHAPTER ELEVEN

THE IMPORTANCE OF FELLOWSHIP IN ESCAPING THE JUDGEMENT OF DELUSION

> exhort one another daily... lest any of you be hardened through the deceitfulness of sin. – Hebrews 3:13

This daily encouragement is a spiritual safeguard that isolates and uproots deception before it takes root. In genuine fellowship with mature believers, there is no room for hidden sin or unchallenged compromise to grow. Instead, every member of the body contributes to keeping hearts sensitive to conviction. When you are known and loved in a Christ-centered community, you cannot drift into delusion unnoticed. Mutual exhortation builds spiritual resilience in a culture that constantly seeks to dull discernment.

The Importance of Fellowship

Walking in the light is not a solitary pursuit. As 1 John 1:7 teaches, *"If we walk in the light... we have fellowship one with another..."* Fellowship rooted in transparency exposes the lies we might otherwise nurse in secret. When you confess struggles and doubts in the safety of godly relationships, shame and deception lose their power. This shared life builds a culture where truth is not simply taught but lived, and where accountability is welcomed rather than feared. In this environment, the seeds of delusion cannot thrive undetected.

An uncompromising church community also protects against the isolation that fuels deception. Satan's strategy has always included separating believers from the body, where their thinking can be distorted without correction. When you commit to biblical fellowship, you place yourself within God's design for your protection. Here, others help you discern truth from error, and you learn to trust God's Word more than your own feelings. This collective vigilance is one of the most effective ways to remain anchored in truth as deception spreads in the last days.

Be Subject to Spiritual Authority

Paul's charge to Timothy underscores the urgency of sound doctrine: *"Preach the word... For the time will come when they will not endure sound doctrine..."* (2 Timothy 4:2–3). A church that faithfully teaches Scripture without compromise provides a steady diet of truth that renews the mind and anchors the heart. In a generation obsessed with novelty and personal truth, expositional preaching confronts deception head-on. When believers gather under clear, consistent teaching, they are equipped to recognize and reject the philosophies that lead to delusion.

Obey them that have the rule over you, and submit yourselves: for they watch for your souls – Hebrews 13:17

Spiritual authority is another vital protection. God-appointed shepherds carry the responsibility to guard doctrine, correct error, and protect the flock from wolves in sheep's clothing. Submitting to this leadership is not about blind loyalty but about recognizing God's provision for your safety. When you live in humble accountability to biblically qualified leaders, you place yourself under spiritual covering that can help you resist the lure of false teaching.

Sound teaching and spiritual authority also cultivate discernment. Instead of relying solely on personal interpretation, believers are trained to test every spirit and hold fast to what is good. This humility in receiving instruction strengthens the conscience and protects the mind from ideas that contradict Christ. Over time, consistent exposure to the whole counsel of God produces stability and maturity that are essential for resisting the subtle encroachment of delusion.

Worship Is Essential

> Let the word of Christ dwell in you richly in all wisdom; teaching and admonishing one another in psalms and hymns and spiritual songs, singing with grace in your hearts to the Lord. - Colossians 3:16

Shared worship is not a passive activity; it is an act of collective warfare against the spirit of the age. When the church gathers to exalt Jesus above all else, idolatry and self-deception are confronted. Singing truth together reinforces doctrine in the heart and renews the mind. This environment strengthens resolve to stand for truth when the world demands compromise.

Corporate worship also keeps the heart tender before God. In the presence of the Holy Spirit, pride is humbled and distractions are cleared away. This spiritual sensitivity is critical for avoiding delusion, which often begins with a loss of reverence and a drift into self-will. When the gathered church fixes its gaze on Christ, the heart is recalibrated to love truth above convenience or cultural approval. In this atmosphere, the deceitfulness of sin loses its allure.

Finally, worship and the pursuit of truth together remind believers that faith is not a private endeavor. Delusion flourishes when people isolate themselves and prioritize personal preference over corporate conviction. In fellowship, believers learn to submit to one another out of reverence for Christ and to hold each other accountable to the gospel. This shared pursuit of holiness, doctrine, and devotion forms a bulwark against the rising tide of deception that marks the last days.

THE STRONG DELUSION

WORKBOOK

A COMPANION STUDY GUIDE FOR REFLECTION, PRAYER, AND DEEPER UNDERSTANDING

Chapter 1: The Psychological View of Delusion

Summary & Key Points

- Delusion is not only spiritual but also a psychological phenomenon defined in DSM-5 as a fixed false belief impervious to reason or evidence.
- Cognitive dissonance (mental discomfort from contradictory beliefs) and ego-protection cause individuals to suppress truth and cling to lies.
- Over time, this suppression can escalate into a reprobate mind—a state of spiritual blindness and moral numbness.
- Delusion becomes judgment when God allows individuals to remain in their self-deception.

Reflection Questions

1. In what ways have you experienced or observed cognitive dissonance in your own beliefs or those of others?
2. Why does the suppression of truth eventually lead to spiritual blindness?
3. What role does pride play in protecting false beliefs?

Scripture for Further Study

"And even as they did not like to retain God in their knowledge, God gave them over to a reprobate mind..."
Romans 1:28

Definitions & Word Study

- Delusion (Greek: πλάνη – *plane*): wandering, deception, error.
- Cognitive Dissonance: mental tension from holding conflicting beliefs.
- Reprobate (Greek: ἀδόκιμος – *adokimos*): unapproved, rejected, unfit.

Devotional

Ask the Lord to show you any area where you have suppressed truth to protect comfort or pride. Pray for courage to face and repent of these areas.

Chapter 2: The Theological View of Delusion

Summary & Key Points

- Delusion arises from rejecting God's truth and choosing self-worship.
- Pride and obstinacy harden the heart and prepare it for spiritual deception.
- Delusion is more than error—it is rebellion against God's authority.
- Like Pharaoh, persistent hardness of heart leads to destruction without remedy.

Reflection Questions

1. How does pride cause people to reinterpret or dismiss God's truth?
2. What examples in modern culture show obstinacy against biblical correction?
3. What does it mean that delusion is a form of idolatry?

Scripture for Further Study

"Pride goeth before destruction, and an haughty spirit before a fall."
Proverbs 16:18

Definitions & Word Study

- Obstinate: stubbornly refusing to change one's opinion or course of action.
- Pride (Hebrew: *ga'own*): arrogance, swelling.
- Idolatry: worship of anything other than God, including self.

Devotional

Reflect on how easily pride can disguise itself as confidence. Surrender any area where you have elevated your own opinions above Scripture.

Chapter 3 – The Sociological View of Delusion

Summary & Key Points

- Delusion spreads through social groups, becoming collective rather than individual.
- Historical examples like the Salem Witch Trials reveal how fear, factionalism, and cultural anxieties fuel mass deception.
- Modern social media and ideology reinforce false beliefs, making delusion feel like community and comfort.
- Collective delusion often masks hidden agendas such as control, power, or personal gain.

Reflection Questions

1. How does social pressure make it harder to recognize deception?
2. Why do people often find comfort in a shared false belief rather than confronting the truth alone?
3. What parallels do you see between past collective delusions and today's cultural movements?

Scripture for Further Study

"This know also, that in the last days perilous times shall come."
2 Timothy 3:1

Definitions & Word Study

- Collective Delusion: A shared false belief held by a group.
- Group think: Conformity of thought within a group.
- Perilous (Greek: *halepos*): dangerous, hard to bear, savage.

Devotional

Reflect on how easily fear can spread through community. Pray for discernment and courage to stand for truth even when it means standing alone.

Chapter 4 – The Satanic Origin of Delusion

Summary & Key Points

- Satan is the father of lies, originating delusion through rebellion and pride.
- His strategy is always to distort God's character and reframe truth as oppression.
- From Eden to modern ideologies, deception hinges on suggesting God withholds something good.
- Lucifer's fall demonstrates the ultimate example of grandiose delusion and self-deification.

Reflection Questions

1. What are the lies Satan whispers today to cause people to doubt God's character?
2. How did pride lead to Lucifer's fall, and how does it lead people into delusion now?
3. Why is self-deification (believing you are your own god) so spiritually dangerous?

Scripture for Further Study

"Ye are of your father the devil...for he is a liar, and the father of it."
John 8:44

Definitions & Word Study

- Delusion (Greek: – *plane*): error, deception, wandering.
- Iniquity (Greek: *anomia*): lawlessness, contempt for divine law.
- Accuser: One who charges with wrongdoing.

Devotional

Consider how subtle lies can reshape your view of God. Ask the Holy Spirit to reveal any deception that has crept into your thinking.

Chapter 5 – The Demonic Role in Delusion

Summary & Key Points

- Demons are intelligent, emotional, and willful beings who enforce lies.
- They create strongholds in the mind by reinforcing false beliefs and resisting truth.
- Ahab's prophets illustrate how demonic spirits exploit willing hearts to spread deception.
- Demons operate hierarchically, targeting minds to keep humanity blind.

Reflection Questions

1. Why is it important to recognize demons as intelligent and strategic, not just chaotic?
2. How do demons use partial truth mixed with lies to create strongholds?
3. What can you learn from Ahab's story about the danger of rejecting truth repeatedly?

Scripture for Further Study

"For we wrestle not against flesh and blood...but against spiritual wickedness in high places."
Ephesians 6:12

Definitions & Word Study

- Stronghold: A fortified belief resistant to truth.
- Skotos: darkness, obscurity.
- Principalities: Ruling spirits assigned to territories.

Devotional

Reflect on the reality of spiritual warfare. Ask God to help you see the hidden battles in your mind and give you courage to stand in His truth.

Chapter 6 – The Demonization of Social Media

Summary & Key Points

- Social media has become a digital pulpit for false doctrines.
- Platforms amplify messages of self-worship and compromise, creating spiritual echo chambers.
- Demons exploit algorithm-driven influence to spread deception more effectively than ever.
- The rise of unaccountable voices with huge followings reveals an end-time fulfillment of prophetic warnings.

Reflection Questions

1. In what ways can social media become a doorway for demonic influence?
2. How can you guard your heart from the subtle reinforcement of unbiblical ideas?
3. Why is it critical to measure teaching by Scripture rather than charisma or popularity?

Scripture for Further Study

"For the time will come when they will not endure sound doctrine..."
2 Timothy 4:3

Definitions & Word Study

- Itching Ears: A craving for teachings that please the listener.
- Doctrine (Greek: *didaché*): teaching, instruction.
- Seducing Spirits: Spirits that entice away from truth.

Devotional

Reflect on the voices you allow to influence you daily. Recommit to filtering every message through the Word of God.

Chapter 7 – Delusion and The Demonization of the Mind

Summary & Key Points

- Delusion begins with persuasion, not possession.
- Repeated rejection of truth creates a reprobate mind incapable of recognizing reality.
- Demons build strongholds of thought, making lies feel like truth and truth feel like hate.
- Imaginations and arguments exalt themselves against the knowledge of God.

Reflection Questions

1. What are some imaginations or arguments you have seen exalted against God's Word?
2. Why does a reprobate mind no longer feel conviction?
3. How does agreement with small lies lead to deeper deception?

Scripture for Further Study

"Casting down imaginations...and bringing into captivity every thought..."
2 Corinthians 10:5

Definitions & Word Study

- Reprobate (Greek: *okimos*): unfit, unapproved, worthless.
- Imaginations: Self-exalting reasonings.
- Stronghold: Fortress of thought that resists truth.

Devotional

Consider any area where you have rationalized sin or deception. Ask God for courage to confront and tear down every stronghold.

Chapter 8 – The Falling Away and the Mystery of Iniquity

Summary & Key Points

- The Falling Away (apostasia) is a deliberate abandonment of truth for comforting lies.
- The Mystery of Iniquity is a hidden system preparing hearts for ultimate deception.
- Rebellion is not passive—it grows into open defiance of God.
- Delusion becomes judgment when people love darkness more than light.

Reflection Questions

1. Why does rejecting truth eventually lead to loving deception?
2. What does the phrase "mystery of iniquity" teach us about hidden spiritual forces?
3. How can you stay anchored in truth when many are falling away?

Scripture for Further Study

"For the mystery of iniquity doth already work..."
2 Thessalonians 2:7

Definitions & Word Study

- Apostasia: rebellion, defection, falling away.
- Iniquity (Greek:*anomia*): lawlessness.
- Deception: The act of making someone believe what is false.

Devotional

Ask the Holy Spirit to keep your heart tender to conviction and rooted in truth, no matter how persuasive deception becomes around you.

BIBLIOGRAPHY

Chapter 1 – The Psychological View of Delusion

Scripture References:

- **Romans 1:18**
- **Romans 1:28**
- **Jeremiah 17:9**
- **1 Timothy 4:2**

Bible Resources:

- American Psychiatric Association, *Diagnostic and Statistical Manual of Mental Disorders*, 5th ed. (Arlington, VA: American Psychiatric Publishing, 2013), 123.
- Leon Festinger, *A Theory of Cognitive Dissonance* (Stanford, CA: Stanford University Press, 1957), 45.
- Aaron T. Beck et al., *Cognitive Therapy of Depression* (New York: Guilford Press, 1979), 55.
- James Strong, *Strong's Expanded Dictionary of Bible Words* (Nashville, TN: Thomas Nelson, 2001), s.v. "Delusion."
- Tyndale House Publishers, *Dictionary of Bible Themes* (Wheaton, IL: Tyndale House, 1999), s.v. "Deception."

Chapter 2 – The Theological View of Delusion

Scripture References:

- **Hebrews 3:15**

- Romans 1:25
- 2 Timothy 3:16
- Proverbs 16:18
- Proverbs 29:1
- Exodus 8:1–15

Bible Resources:

- Matthew Henry, *Commentary on the Whole Bible* (Peabody, MA: Hendrickson Publishers, 1991), Exodus 8.
- Thomas Nelson Publishers, *Life in the Spirit Study Bible* (Grand Rapids, MI: Zondervan, 1992), note on Proverbs 16:18.

Chapter 3 – The Sociological View of Delusion

Scripture References:

- Exodus 22:18
- 2 Timothy 3:1–5
- 1 Timothy 4:1

Bible Resources:

1. Barna Group, *The State of the Church 2020* (Ventura, CA: Barna Group, 2020), 15.
2. Pew Research Center, *In U.S., Decline of Christianity Continues at Rapid Pace* (Washington, DC: Pew Research Center, 2019), 6.
3. Gallup, "LGBT Identification in U.S. Ticks Up to 7.1%," February 17, 2022, https://news.gallup.com/poll/389792/lgbt-identification-ticks-up.aspx.

4. **Tyndale House Publishers.**
   Dictionary of Bible Themes. Wheaton, IL: Tyndale House, 1999.

Chapter 4 – The Satanic Origin of Delusion

Scripture References:

- John 8:44
- Isaiah 14:12–15
- Ezekiel 28:12–15
- Luke 10:18
- Genesis 3:1–5
- Revelation 12:10
- Job 1:1–11

Bible Resources:

1. Thomas Nelson Publishers, *Life in the Spirit Study Bible*, note on Isaiah 14.
2. James Strong, *Strong's Expanded Dictionary of Bible Words*, s.v. "Lucifer."

Chapter 5 – The Demonic Role in Delusion

Scripture References:

- **1 Kings 22:22**
- **Luke 4:33–34**
- **James 2:19**
- **Matthew 8:29**

- Matthew 12:43–44
- Ephesians 6:12
- John 3:19
- 2 Timothy 4:3

Bible Resources:

1. Thomas Nelson Publishers, *Life in the Spirit Study Bible*, note on Luke 4.

Chapter 6 – The Demonization of Social Media

Scripture References:

- 1 Timothy 4:1–2
- Genesis 3:5
- 2 Timothy 4:3

Bible Resources:

1. Pew Research Center, *Religious Landscape Study* (Washington, DC: Pew Research Center, 2014), 7.
2. Barna Group, *New Age Spirituality in the Church* (Ventura, CA: Barna Group, 2020), 10.

Chapter 7 – Delusion and the Demonization of the Mind

Scripture References:

- Romans 1:28
- 1 Timothy 4:2

- **2 Timothy 3:13**
- **2 Corinthians 10:4–5**
- **Romans 1:22–27**

Bible Resources:

1. Gallup, *U.S. Church Membership Falls Below Majority* (Washington, DC: Gallup, 2022), 3.
2. James Strong, *Strong's Expanded Dictionary of Bible Words*, s.v. "Mind."

Chapter 8 – The Falling Away and the Mystery of Iniquity

Scripture References:

- **2 Thessalonians 2:3, 7, 11**
- **Matthew 24:12**
- **Romans 1:25**
- **Jeremiah 2:13**
- **Judges 21:25**
- **2 Timothy 4:3**
- **2 Timothy 2:17–18**
- **2 Timothy 4:10**

Bible Resources:

1. Barna Group, *The State of Theology Survey* (Ventura, CA: Barna Group, 2020), 12.
2. Pew Research Center, *In U.S., Decline of Christianity Continues at Rapid Pace*, 7.

Chapter 9 – The Word Made Flesh

Scripture References:

- John 1:1–3, 14
- Hebrews 1:1–3
- Colossians 1:15–17
- Isaiah 55:8
- John 14:6
- 2 Corinthians 4:4
- Revelation 12:9
- Genesis 3:1

Bible Resources:

1. James Strong, *Strong's Expanded Dictionary of Bible Words*, s.v. "Logos."
2. Tyndale House Publishers, *Dictionary of Bible Themes*, s.v. "Incarnation."

Chapter 10 – Escaping the Judgment of Delusion

Scripture References:

- 2 Thessalonians 2:10–11
- Romans 12:2
- Ephesians 4:23
- 2 Corinthians 10:5
- 1 John 1:7
- 2 Corinthians 13:5

- Proverbs 9:8
- John 14:6

Bible Resources:

1. Tyndale House Publishers, *Dictionary of Bible Themes*, s.v. "Renewal."

Chapter 11 – The Importance of Fellowship

Scripture References:

- Hebrews 3:13
- 1 John 1:7
- 2 Timothy 4:2–3
- Hebrews 13:17
- Colossians 3:16

Bible Resources:

1. Matthew Henry, *Commentary on the Whole Bible*, Hebrews 3.
2. Thomas Nelson Publishers, *Life in the Spirit Study Bible*, note on Colossians

www.ingramcontent.com/pod-product-compliance
Lightning Source LLC
Chambersburg PA
CBHW070044230426
43661CB00005B/747